Dedicated
my family a

With special thanks to Pete Bingley
for making this book of street
poems possible

A Banger In Belgrave Hospital

When I was asked to write a book of poetry by my good mate Pete, my first thought was to issue song lyrics from the many cds I've made over the years as a musician and Singer/Songwriter.
I decided instead to write a book of poetry based on my early childhood and teenage years growing up on the Streatham vale estate on the southern most tip of the London borough of Lambeth.
Streatham vale was originally known as Lonesome before the estate was built and was the home of highwaymen and was a forboding place.

A lot of the poems are based on family stories which I grew up with as a child; growing up in post war London in the 1950s and still on rationing.. If you was lucky you had a one channel tv set with a nine inch screen that was always breaking down.. A bush radio set that used to crackle and the sheer joy of hearing a rock and roll song.

Without too much more explanation I would rather let the book speak for itself.

Arthur Kitchener, 2015

The Father I knew

You believed in god and country the same beliefs as mine
And had no hesitation when you signed on the dotted line
You rose to bombardier and your friends believed in you
The father the father that I knew

You stood side by side to keep the enemy from the door
And bravely made a stand in the battle of Singapore
And that spirit it lives on in our heroes passing through
The father the father that I knew

You made it back home with my mother you was one
I remember the day she told me all the bravery you done

A war widows pension that's all my mother had
And a couple of black and white photos
To remind me of my dad
And that spirit it lives on in our heroes passing through
The father the father that I knew

How many years have passed how many years have gone?
Will we ever learn as the battle still rages on?
Freedom must be fought for
And I believe that too
The father the father that I knew

GVI RI

This scroll commemorates

Bombardier A. P. Kitchener
Royal Regiment of Artillery

held in honour as one who
served King and Country in
the world war of 1939-1945
and gave his life to save
mankind from tyranny. May
his sacrifice help to bring
the peace and freedom for
which he died.

Young Kennedy

Old grandfather Percy was a boxer in his day
He always went the distance or so my dear old mum would say
He was scared of no man from Tottenham came he
Who fought under the name of young Kennedy

In Blackfriars ring young Kennedy would fight
Crowds from all over London came when it was boxing night
My mother said he lost more fights that he did ever win
And when he won the door came off and let the whole street in

Mum and dad stood in a crowd to watch the king go past
Outside the houses of parliament crowds gathered to the last
Bold as brass strolled percy with 2 rabbits he did strut
Down the centre of the road he just got from the cut

Percy never made it to the boxing hall of fame
He died before I knew him his legend I maintain
From a generation life war really tough you see
Boxing was a poor mans out for young Kennedy

Made in England

I was five and you was four
You was my friend who lived next door
We was constantly at war
With the kids from every other street and avenue

Just a river kept our gangs apart
We was the best we was smart
When they crossed they had to yield
Their side of the river was another world

So don't cross the river you must always stay your side
Stand up and be counted and never run and hide
When you think of where you came from
It must fill your heart with pride
Knowing that you was made in England

At the age of five I started school
They taught me all there have to rules
For queen and country I must fight
But fighting in the playground is not right at all

The heroes home praise be to god
What I never understood
Why is my mother all alone
And is my daddy ever coming home

You can find employment if your hands are skilled
Don't trust in your leaders they can get you killed
Its what you give is what you get that's how the cards are dealed
The reason is that you was made in England

And if the country needs you you'll have to go to war
You're here because your here lad you're here because you're poor
And there aint no work in England so what you crying for
While Joe your son is hanging round street corners in London
Selling hooky motors and having lots of fun
So we'll stick a medal on your chest for the bravery you did
You can sell it down the porn shop if you're short of a few quid

The teenage years are now no more
So marry the girl who lives next door
To raise our kids to fight the kids
Who live on every other street and avenue?

Still divided after all this time
Doing what we're told towing the line
Why does it have to be this way
Putting the world to rights is how we have our say

You can count your blessings if you have a council home
If you can't pay the mortgage you're out there all alone
And don't forget to tell us if you choose to roam
And praise the lord that you was made in England

Clowns of The Lambeth walk

My Great grand dad was a travelling clown
From Italy he came
And settled off the Lambeth walk
In search of fortune and fame
When they fled from Italy somewhere along the line
They changed from Garto in to Gatty
To them that was just fine

There was Henry and harry father and son
A clown act they did call
Henry was the white clown
Harry the Auguste fool
When Theresa and Annie came along
In music halls they made a stand
The greatest music act that ever crossed the land

The four musical Gartos
The crowds really enjoyed
As they toured country to country
With Harry Lauder and Marie Lloyd
From city town to city the family would tour
When they went to Russia the crowds cried out for more

They lined up all their guineas
Round the table when they came home
And basked in all their fortune
From where they did perform
When the show was over they still had to eat
And sadly took their instruments
To the pawn shop down the street

I don't know the last show
My mother never said
They never got the recognition
That their contemporaries had
The little band of travelling clowns
In their day they made a stand
The four musical Gartos were the greatest in the land

Harry Gatty

Henry and Harry Gatty

The ride to rotten row

There's a place in Hyde Park the nobility would go
They rode there horses up and down
A walk called rotten row
Far removed from our world
The one in which we lived
On the other side of the river
Across the Lambeth bridge
Mum lived in a terrace house
Just off the Lambeth walk
A lad called Cobbie Betson
Who my mum would often talk
He asked the rag and bone man
If he could walk his horse
The rag and bone man smiled
That's kind of you of course
Cobbie took the horse together
Crossed the Lambeth Bridge
He wanted to show the nobility
Who he was and what he did
He made his mark in Hyde Park
And let the gentry know
I'm just as good as you as he rode on Rotten Row

Mum, Nan, and Uncle Jack, who lied about his age in WW1.
He survived

Yer Dear old Mother

There's no one in the world like yer dear old mother
You can go out east go out west
But you'll never find another
She'll get yer bail when you get yer collar felt
And say my sons a good boy and butter wouldn't melt

There's no one in the world like yer dear old mother
She give you a roof that's the truth
Somewhere to recover
She'll bring in your cigarettes
when yer banged up in clink
And throw a blanket over you
when yer the worse for drink

There's no one in the world like yer dear old mother
You'll never get another one
So cherish her and love her
When the odds are stacked against yer
And yer feeling glum
Remember There's no one else like yer dear old mum

Mum and Dad

A Banger In Belgrave Hospital

Around the time of Guy Fawkes Night
I thought Guy Fawkes was really cool
When the powers that be forced me to see
A doctor who took me for a fool

Your son they said is maladjusted
The little toe rag can't be trusted
All he does is run away
And punches a boxing bag all day

He assembles toys back to front
Life to him's a cunning stunt
Send him away it's for the best
Society deserves a well earned rest

Back home I plotted my revenge
Like Guy Fawkes I would avenge
Before they stretched me on the rack
With a tuppeny banger I would attack

I sat with other kids like me
I told my mother I had to wee
And in the quiet W.C
I placed my banger carefully

I lit the fuse made my retreat
And returned quickly to my seat
And in the silence my heart it sang
As I waited for the bang

And bang it did it must be said
Then I got a clout around my head
Was it worth it after all?
Yes Guy Fawkes was really cool

The Ballad Of Derek Bentley

Two young boys one night they made the scene
One was Derek Bentley the wrong side of seventeen
Craig the other said lets go and have some fun
Bentley did not know that Craig he had a gun
They climbed a roof just to see what they could get
The old bill was watching they had them in the net
Bentley said I've had enough
And gave him up when the going got too tough

You never said this
LET HIM HAVE IT CHRIS you just let them take you down

Up on the roof nobody told the truth
How Bentley gave assistance instead of resistance
Fair cop guv that's all you had to say
While Chris Craigs gun was blasting fast away
You gave yourself up surrendered to the crown
You never told Craig to shoot that copper down

Nine bells is all you're going to get
A cup of coffee and a last cigarette
There's those who say that you threw your life away
But I can't hear one single word they say
You gave your life that's all you had to give
You had to die so that others can live
As you spend your last hour in jail
Sadly your mates walk the streets of Streatham vale

You never said this
LET HIM HAVE IT CHRIS you just let them take you down

Holidays In Herne Bay

Holidays in Herne bay when I was a kid
Fishing off the pier end that is what we did
A line of London coaches lined up at the pier
We stayed in dockland settlement which it was quite near

I'd have my bowl of cockles then would make my way
Down to the arcades on one armed bandits I would play
A line of pin ball machines buckaroo and aces high
To get another replay I would always try

In a smoke filled public house my mum would disappear
And bring me out crisps and coke when she went for a beer
In those long hot summer days I would play for hours
With other kids at Bishopstone glen and Reculver towers

Sometimes mum and I would stroll to Hampton pier
For her it was a long walk to me it was quite near
She'd sit for hours on the beach for me it was just fine
I'd fill a bucket up with crabs that I'd caught on a line

Then we'd go for coffee in Macaris restaurant
I would feed the jukebox till my pocket money gone
To me it was another world a week of simple fun
The holiday was over as fast as it begun

We got back on the coach with another tale
And headed back to London and dear old Streatham vale
When we got back home with my mates I'd go and play
And tell them all that happened on holiday in Herne Bay

The Battle Of Danbrook Road

Beyond the fog and London smog on the edge of Lonesome town
The bombsites and bomb buildings were our battleground
We threw rocks at each other our battle song we sang
You had to have a track bike to be a member of our gang

Remember when the boy's brigade grabbed Danny going home
They roughed him up took no account that he weren't on his own
When he said what happened our anger did explode
Vengeance would be ours if the BB marched down Danbrook Road

We turned up on our bikes each and every one
Dressed like Marlon Brando in the wild one
The kids from Colmer and Danbrook road and one from Lonesome town
Right to the last they shall not pass or bully us around

The word went out on the streets the boy's brigade would march
Right past Saint Bartholomew's with their drums and brass
We gathered on our bombsite knowing they would scoff and goad
Only god can save them if they march down Danbrook road

The sound of silence filled the air you could read on every face
Then nipper shouts they're coming get yer track bikes all in place
The drums and brass got louder wheel to wheel and toe to toe
In rows we lined our bikes right across Danbrook road

Outside Saint Bartholomew was wondering the score
The boy's brigade marched right past not knowing what's in store
The major shouted left wheel like clockwork to and fro
Then see our track bike barricade across old Danbrook road

But still they marched right on towards our track bike barricade
The major shouts out of the way a tuneless march they played
We just swore at em all and firmly held the line
I shouted you can shove yer brass where the sun don't shine

The BB marched in to us that is what they did
Their band was getting quiet as a human pyramid
Of drums and brass and bikes and kids and angry swearing mums
I laughed as my cow horn handlebars went through their big bass drum

That's where the music ended in the middle of the street
We pulled back our bikes and cheered as the BB did retreat
They never marched up there again I had to let you know
Life went on as normal down on Danbrook road

The Four Musical Garto's on tour

Me, a young rocker. 1963

Aunt Lizzie

Aunt Lizzie was my favourite aunt, who lived down Walworth way
A big old house in Sutherland square where I would often stay
I would buy 5 woodbines, winkle pickers on my feet
I'd stroll down the Walworth road to the market in East Street

Aunt Lizzie had a lodger, Bill it was his name
He would tell Millwall story's when he went to Cold Blow lane
He promised he would take me and that filled my every thought
And with a name like Kitchener who else could I support

I lived closer to the palace than the mighty den
My mother was a Lambeth girl I'd fight my cause again
Selhurst park it aint that far please listen to my plea
May be 2 miles closer but a million culturally

Lizzie had a cuckoo clock that came out on a spring
My mother's brother waited for the bell to ring
The cuckoo came right out then he grabbed it in its track
The cuckoo never came out again or ever did go back

Aunt Lizzies son got boxing gloves on one Christmas day
He went out in the square with the other kids to play
A copper knocked on Lizzie's door and said, 'what's happening here'
He's bashing all the other kids, Lizzie clipped him round the ear

Aunt Lizzie told a story about her husband Jack
A First World War telegram said he's missing and not back
Heartbroken went in mourning in black from head to toe
And went to do her shopping down the Walworth road did go

The story didn't end there Aunt Lizzie she would tell
Jack walked towards her in the square and said 'hello old girl'
I made it here's me medal what a wonderful surprise
She gave him a right hander then tears filled in her eyes

That was my great aunt Lizzie a legend that's no doubt
She lived to 93 with her pint of stout
When I went back home there was something in my coat
She hugged me in my pocket there was a ten bob note

The Wanderer

In the spring of 1962 the twist was all the craze
To the cinema i went on one of those lazy days
The film was twist around the clock
The Greatest song I heard
The song it was The Wanderer I took in every word

It hit me like a thunderbolt Life would never be the same
I had found myself a mentor and Dion is his name
His songs gave me direction his songs they shone a light
And in My darkest hour his book helped save my life

With Del Shannon and Joe Brown the tour hit London Town
Inside Tooting Granada Outside I hung around
I was too young to get in for money I was poor
When you sang The Wanderer my ear pressed to the door

My birthday came with the greatest present ever got
A small record player to the record shop I shot
With my pocket money to the record shop i ran
Bought The Wanderer and got it home my life had just began

The sound of the stylus when the needle kissed the disc
When the record started I was in rock n roll bliss
I played over and over my heart it sang with pride
And played The Majestic on the other side

My mate Pete he gave me on top rank Runaround Sue
I saved for Little Diane and Lovers who wander too
I bought love came to me Sandy had me in a whirl
Drip Drop Ruby baby Donna prima Donna and This little girl

At a records stand over in Earls court
Your singles with The Belmont's Back catalogue I bought
And when Beatle mania swept across all the UK
With my box of Dion records i would go my way

As the years roll on with a bass i made my stand
And got to tour myself with many a great band
when the DJs ask me for me all-time greatest song
I always say The Wanderer that's where it all came from

Dion and me

The Sound Of The Shapes

Tuesday was a great night from what I can recall
And meet up with my mates in the holy redeemer hall
Once we was all talking someone said lets form a band
And on that dusty stage we can make our stand

Steve Herbert was our drummer and a local face
Clive played lead guitar as I struggled on the bass
Brian also played guitar and Ian was our voice
We called ourselves the shapes and all agreed the choice

Sunday afternoon band practise round my place
Mother would come in with some tea and cakes
Planning the big night when we would give it all
In front of all the mod girls in the holy redeemer hall

The local mods and modettes came from near and far
Classic sixties songs was our repertoire
All five on that stage standing just like brothers
Songs like keep on running and classic motown covers

All those weeks of playing was over far too soon
The shapes they were born in that dusty room
In the local youth clubs we played our set around
And in the Streatham ice rink we played search for a sound

For us it was the big one and meant so much to me
We played along the Sonics and me and my three
Those memories still with me 5 lads who made a stand
On the holy redeemer stage the shapes it was the band

Me with violin bass, Streatham Ice Rink, 1967

November 14th 1881
BRITANNIA MUSIC HALL
Pre-eminently the most popular place of amusement

THE UNRIVALLED LADY COMIQUE
MISS BESSIE BELLWOOD

November 19th 1881
Dezmonti & Mora
The greatest double bar artistes extant.
Testo and Mdlle. Onri,
Marvelous American Atheletes
Picard, the boy comique

November 28th 1881
Special engagement from the 'Oxford' London
Of Vento Vento!!
The great ventriloquist and mechanical manipulator Vento
is supported by an immense company
Dezmonti & Mora
Testo & Onri
Mr & Mrs J. Drew
Lizzie Watson
and others of music hall supremacy tonight.

Demember 16th 1881
W.J. Ashcroft, the great original solid man,
Supported by the Immense company comprising
THE MARVELOUS GARTO'S
The Greatest Musical Genius of the age
Mino the Marvel
and more

The bill from Britannia Music Hall, 1881

The River Graveney

You've heard of the Mississippi and the river Thames
And all the mighty rivers that begins and never ends
There's a little river that means a lot to me
Runs through part of south London called the river Graveney

It starts somewhere in Addiscombe in Norbury is a brook
In a concrete basin it don't get a second look
Through the heart of lonesome to amen corner running free
Then joins the river Wandle to the Thames and estuary

We forced the railings far apart climb down its banks and play
And dam it up like beavers with anything that came our way
When it was raining hard the river rose so high
And the rubbish dumped in to it quickly did flow by

The riverside gang of seven wondered where it all began
And crawled through the bogey tunnel and tried to not fall in
I never see a fish or eel swim through that murky haze
A duck swam on it once and we talked of it for days

As the years rolled by with my motorbike I'd play
Then Roger from the gale in our box room he did stay
Then my dear old mother said you two should have a think
Get rid of those two armchairs to me it's worth a drink

When mum disappeared in to the fog we wasn't going to slack
We carried out the armchairs through the alley round the back
The river flowing fast the river flowing high
We soaked them both in petrol before we watched them sail by

In flames they sailed towards the bridge to Roger I did say
They look just like two fire ships back in Nelsons day
What we never reckoned as we stood before the mast
Mother was standing on the bridge and watched them sail past

When she got back home she yelled come out here you two
I know what you been doing I got a bone to pick with you
Her anger turned to laughter she looked at Rog and me
And said I will forgive you if you make a cup of tea

Well that's the river Graveney to us it was just fun
With its network of alleyways to hide when on the run
The river is still flowing from its tiny well
Now there's other generations with stories they can tell

Stroll On Zigger Zagger Kitchener

There's a legend from cold blow lane
Barry Kitchener is his name
For 6.0.2 games he went
And always gave one hundred percent
He made himself a career
Of filling opposition up with fear

When other clubs they offered fame
You stuck with the lions of cold blow lane
Turned your back on Liverpool
And gave it all for Millwall
Good and bad times you came through
And should have gone up in 72

A lion in a lion's shirt
It never showed when you was hurt
And when they tried to drag our name
You stuck with the lions of cold blow lane
Always played with great control
Powerful headers bang on goal

Stroll on zigger zagger Kitchener
Stroll on zigger zagger Kitchener
A Millwall legend is what you are
Stroll on zigger zagger Kitchener

Barry Kitchener and me

Clerkenwell

Clerkenwell has always been a special place to me
And once was home for many an Italian family
My home was a small bedsit in Wilmington square
I could walk in to the west end in 20 minutes from there

Just a small box room from what I can recall
With an Athena poster covering the wall
Early every morning to work off I would go
As a leather worker at a place in Colebrook row

Lunch was in Alfredos round the corner I would stroll
They was filming Quadrophenia when I popped in for a roll
And in a small brown envelope my wages were in cash
Then down to Exmouth market for double pie and mash

I really loved my room in Wilmington square
And many of my first songs I wrote while living there
Walking past Saint Peters they would ring the Angelis Bell
Just some memories when I lived in Clerkenwell

Great, great Grandfather, Frederic Gatty- artist.
Noted for painting a ceiling in Walnut Tree Walk,
Lambeth.

Barnes Wallis Went To Millwall

Barnes Wallis went to Millwall
on that I have no doubt
Its where he learnt what football
was really all about
and on those crowded terraces
... he watched again and again
It was only a short distance
From his house to cold blow lane

Barnes Wallis went to Millwall
On that I can tell you now
After drinking light and bitters
Back in the dun cow
Till he got hit by a long ball
Well the hell did that come from
And in his New Cross garden
Developed the bouncing bomb

Barnes Wallis went to Millwall
On that I sure can tell
With his friend Guy Gibson
And his dog as well
On the beaches of Reculver
He shed a tiny tear
As he watched his Bouncing Bomb
Take out Herne Bay Pier

Barnes Wallis went to Millwall
That's where he Learnt to Sing
With Arthur Bomber Harris
And the entire Duxford wing
Next time you see a Long ball
Reaching for the sky
Barnes Wallis went to Millwall
And that's the Reason why.

Street Poet

I stood behind him on a stage once

Not in a club or in a bar

But on the back of a trailer

A make shift stage for the carnival star

The man he introduced him

And said we got a band to play

But first we got a poet

Then the band is underway

He put a hand in a pocket

Of a worn out army coat

Pulled out a piece of paper

Into a mike he softly spoke

The crowd was getting restless

They could not under stand

The talent of the poet

They were there to hear the band

The crowd had come to hear the music

The crowd had come to watch the band

They joked about the tramp street poet

Whose words they did not understand

We was there for the free beer and a little company

On his own with a microphone he gave it away for free

Just an old street poet

Trying to be heard

You say nobody listened

But I took in every word

He climbed down from the trailer stage

Drank a drink and sighed a sigh

Then stumbled through a growing crowd

Of apathetic passers by

I tried to say a few words

Before I sang my song

By the time I hit my first note

The poet he had gone

Willie The Buddha And Me

Many years ago I tried to make a stand
With a member of the animals in a rock n roll band
I said I want to make it and wonder why I can't
In the back of my song book who wrote a Buddhist chant

I joined a local Buddhist group that's just what I did
I must have driven my poor wife mad along with all my kids
Looking back on it now it all seemed quite a laugh
But when it broke my marriage it also broke my heart in half

My good friend Peter took my mate George and me
To a meeting down in Sussex and not far from the sea
When we finally got there the meeting had a theme
Which was a reason to be cheerful to me that was a dream?

We sat on a table with a geezer who's in charge
He had a fixed smile and eyes that were quite large
His manner was a graceful swan gliding on a lake
But underneath was paddling hard to stay up no mistake

He fixed his stare right on me and asked if I could find
A reason to be cheerful and the first thought in my mind
Without hesitation without being lead
Wee Willie Harris and that is what I said

I see by his expression that he looked bemused
So I told my little story not trying to confuse
I come from Streatham vale one of rock n rolls elite
Wee Willie Harris lived right across the street

Wee Willie Harris Tommy Steele and Terry Dene
Where right there at the start when rock n roll burst on the scene
At the 2 I's coffee bar was where it all began
The greatest music I had heard soon swept across the land

I told him about the teddy boys and every teenage cult
His smile now was changing how you got that result
Reasons to be cheerful that's an Ian Drury song
And the theme of your meeting that's where I got it from

Trembling now he said that's true I cannot see why
Wee Willie Harris is in the forefront of your mind
I said play the song again after weekends in Paris
The next line Ian Drury said was wee Willie Harris

I enjoyed the food and it really was a shame
That he never looked my way or asked me anything again
I really enjoyed the meeting down in Sussex by the sea
It brought a smile to my face Willie the Buddha and me

You Aint Playing On Our Show You Aint

You aint playing on our show you aint
The way they let you know is often quite quaint
That's if they have the courtesy
To let you know at all
You check your mobile daily
For a message or lost call
Between you and your audience
Is a mile high brick wall
You aint playing on our show you aint

You aint playing our festival you're not
We know just who you are and the band you got
You need to speak to Giles
Hes in a meeting and not here
Send us in a sound byte
We are never going to hear
Try and contact us again
The same time and next year
You aint playing our festival you're not

You aint playing our pub and that's a no no
We don't care about your records on the radio
The bands you formed are touring
That really is a shame
The people that once loved you
Wont book you back again
And all your work and effort
Is going down the drain
You aint playing in our pub and that's a no no

The Queen Of Mount Carmel

Holy Mother Mary wont you shine your light on me
I ain't been much a father to my family
I seen that light in other men's eyes the loving that they feel
Please let me feel that way
The queen of Mount Carmel

I knelt before your statues tears pouring from my eyes
I'm right out of excuses and drunken alibis
I squandered all my money and lie and cheat and steal
Holy mother forgive me
The queen of Mount Carmel

I said I'd stand my ground when I had to fight
With the big book in my left hand and a guitar in my right
I was living in cloud cuckoo land the stories I would tell
Holy mother forgive me
The queen of Mount Carmel

Now my years are passing and the truth has set me free
I thought my songs would change things but that was fantasy
Only one thing I ask when on my knees I kneel
Protect my friends and family
The queen of Mount Carmel

The Isle Of Avalon

There's a place that I belong called the isle of Avalon
Where the buzzards soar above the tor and the air is filled with song
It's the only place I want to be a place where I feel really free
So free in Avalon

I want to live a life of peace and the war in me to cease
I want to make amends to the friends for any wrongs I have released
And hear the stories that they tell about the chalice and the well
So free in Avalon

From the dawn of creation you've been a spark of inspiration
I can feel the love in me starting to rise
When I am weak you make me strong this is the land that I belong
And when far away I realise

Lay me down upon the tor and let my spirit soar
When my race is run I can return back to the land that I adore
And sing the songs that I have sung across the fields of Avalon
So free in Avalon